Richard Chenevix Trench

**Sermons Preached Before the University of Cambridge**

Richard Chenevix Trench

**Sermons Preached Before the University of Cambridge**

ISBN/EAN: 9783337160968

Printed in Europe, USA, Canada, Australia, Japan

Cover: Foto ©Lupo / pixelio.de

More available books at **www.hansebooks.com**

# SERMONS.

*Works by* R. C. TRENCH, D.D., *Dean of Westminster.*
IN UNIFORM STYLE WITH THIS VOLUME.

### I.
### ON THE STUDY OF WORDS.
NEW AND REVISED EDITION.
1 vol. 12mo. Price 75 cents.

### II.
### ON THE LESSONS IN PROVERBS.
1 vol. 12mo. Price 50 cents.

### III.
### SYNONYMS OF THE NEW TESTAMENT.
1 vol. 12mo. Price 75 cents.

### IV.
### ON THE ENGLISH LANGUAGE
PAST AND PRESENT.
1 vol. 12mo. Price 75 cents.

### V.
### POEMS.
1 vol. Price one dollar.

### VI.
### CALDERON, HIS LIFE AND GENIUS.
WITH SPECIMENS OF HIS PLAYS.
1 vol. 12mo. Price 75 cents.

### VII.
### SERMONS ON THE DIVINITY OF CHRIST
1 vol. 12mo. Price 50 cents.

### VIII.
### ON THE AUTHORIZED VERSION OF THE NEW TESTAMENT,
IN CONNECTION WITH RECENT PROPOSALS FOR ITS REVISION.
1 vol. 12mo. Price 75 cents.

### IX.
### A SELECT GLOSSARY OF ENGLISH WORDS, USED FORMERLY IN SENSES DIFFERENT FROM THEIR PRESENT.
1 vol. 12mo. Price 75 cents.

### X.
### SERMONS PREACHED IN WESTMINSTER ABBEY.
1 vol. 12mo. Price one dollar.

PUBLISHED BY W. J. WIDDLETON, NEW YORK.

# SERMONS

PREACHED BEFORE

## THE UNIVERSITY OF CAMBRIDGE

BY

RICHARD CHENEVIX TRENCH, D.D.

DEAN OF WESTMINSTER

AUTHOR OF "SYNONYMS OF THE NEW TESTAMENT"—"THE STUDY OF WORDS"—
"ENGLISH, PAST AND PRESENT"—"PROVERBS"—"POEMS"—"CALDERON," ETC

NEW YORK
W. J. WIDDLETON
SUCCESSOR TO J. S. REDFIELD
1862

# CONTENTS.

### SERMON I.
CHRIST THE ONLY BEGOTTEN OF THE FATHER . . PAGE 7

### SERMON II.
CHRIST THE LAMB OF GOD . . . . . . . . . . . 35

### SERMON III.
CHRIST THE LIGHT OF THE WORLD . . . . . . . 63

### SERMON IV.
CHRIST THE TRUE VINE . . . . . . . . . . . 87

### SERMON V.
CHRIST THE JUDGE OF ALL MEN . . . . . . . . 113

# SERMON I.

## CHRIST THE ONLY BEGOTTEN OF THE FATHER.

# SERMON I.

## CHRIST THE ONLY BEGOTTEN OF THE FATHER.

JOHN i. 1, 14.

In the beginning was the Word, and the Word was with God, and the Word was God. . . . . . And the Word was made flesh, and dwelt among us (and we beheld his glory, the glory as of the only begotten of the Father), full of grace and truth.

ALL the controversies of our time, whatever questions are stirring at any depth the minds and spirits of men, concentrate themselves more and more around the person of Christ. "What think ye of Christ?" is more and more *the* question, which according as we answer, we shall answer every other question; for it rules and determines the answers to all. This fact, which few, I imagine, would dispute, must not be regarded as one auguring ill for the present condition of that long conflict of faith with unbelief, which in one shape or another runs throughout all ages, and lies at the root of so many subordinate conflicts which at first sight appear to be remote from it. It is not as though, after all the outworks had fallen, after these had one by one been assailed and taken, the defenders of some beleaguered town were yet defending the citadel to the last, knowing that its loss would be the loss of all, that after it, nothing more remained to defend. It is rather as when, after the tide of battle has long been swaying uncertainly hither and thither, the insight of the captains on either side, or the very instincts of the combatants themselves, have led them to perceive the point where victory is to be seized, or defeat to be averted; the true key of the position contended for; that which, as it is won, everything will be won, no petty losses elsewhere affecting this result; that which, as it is lost, everything will be lost, no slight successes in any other quarter at all availing to redress the balance, or give back the victory which has been lost.

I have, then — not indeed in any presumptuous hope to add aught here to what others have already spoken, yet still under the influence of these convictions — chosen for my argument during the month that I shall address you from this place, subjects which all directly treat of the person and dignities of our Lord; which treat of what he claims, or what Scripture claims *for* him, to be. Without pretending to any very strict order of sequence or coherence, they yet will not be wholly without this. They will all grow out of that central dignity, Word of God, Only begotten of the Father, which is about to occupy us this day; and, with the exception of this day's discourse, they will all be suggested by the services of the Sundays on which they are delivered. As to-day we have to do with the witness of John the Evangelist to his Lord, so, next Sunday, I propose, God willing, to deal with the witness of the other John to Jesus, " Behold the Lamb of God, which taketh away the sin of the world;" and then, in my remaining discourses, with the Lord's witness, under three aspects, to himself: as the Light of the world, as the True Vine, and, lastly, on Advent Sunday, as the Judge of all men, to whom all judgment is committed, because he is the Son of Man. May he of his own grace, give a mouth and wisdom to speak only right things of him.

By a course not altogether unusual, I have, omitting the intermediate verses, connected the first verse of the Gospel of St. John with the fourteenth, making these to serve for my text; and I have done this not without special reason. For how often the Gospel of St. John practically begins for us at this fourteenth verse, " The Word was made flesh, and dwelt among us, full of grace and truth," or a verse or two earlier, at the very earliest. All that goes before, as we freely admit, must have its purpose and value, since God has been pleased to reveal it; but still for us we feel its chief value to be that with it we can stop the mouths of Unitarians,

or of those, rather, who call themselves such;
that it proves one of the most available weapons
of controversy for the refutation of *their* errors,
and all those other errors, Arian and the like,
which in the end inevitably flow into theirs.
These are the chief purposes which that sublime
prologue to the fourth Gospel, that fitting vestibule to this augustest temple, that portion of
Scripture which more than any other stirred the
marvel and admiration of the philosophical
heathen, and drew one and another within the
charmed circle of Christian truth, very often
seems to us as though it were intended to serve.
It invites us to no earnest meditation; we do
not seek to lose ourselves in its wondrous depths,
that we may find ourselves again at heights of
which we dreamed not before; we make little or
no attempt to place the loftier speculation of our
own day in relation and subordination to it.
The Incarnation is for us the beginning of the
history of Christ—his Sonship itself practically,
I do not say theoretically, beginning for us from
that date. We should reject, perhaps with some-

thing of indignation, any such statement, if it were put boldly before us. And yet how often Christ is regarded as the Word of God, because he then, in the days of his flesh, uttered his Father's word to the children of men; the Wisdom of God, because of the wisdom manifested in the carrying out of our redemption; the Image of God, because he that hath seen him hath seen the Father.

We have not, indeed, in the least denied that he was Son, and Word, and Wisdom, and Image, by an earlier right, by one which is out of, and removed from, all conditions of time. The fact, as revealed, we dutifully accept. But still we do not perceive how this glory of Christ which he had with the Father before all worlds, very closely concerns us or our salvation. It gradually falls farther and farther back in our minds; our lively interest in theology only commencing with the Word made flesh, as though then first man's close connection with God began; whereas, indeed, it dates from the creation, or rather from the divine purpose of the creation — the

Incarnation being not the cause and root out of which that connection springs, but rather itself the result and consequence thereof, the crowning flower into which in due time that relation unfolded itself. Nay, sometimes even the Incarnation itself is felt as a step too early, and it is the Atonement which first greatly occupies our thoughts, or deeply stirs our affections.

Let us beware, brethren, lest we allow selfishness to intrude into a region where least of all it should find place, but which yet too easily may become its especial haunt and home; so that we shall measure the value of truths, not by the utterance which they contain of God's attributes, his wisdom, his love, his righteousness, his truth, not by the glory which they bring to him, but solely by the bearing which they seem to have on ourselves, and on our own individual spiritual life. Something of this kind may perhaps be traced among us now; when the truths for which Augustine struggled, the doctrines of grace, are still precious and dear to us, because they seem to bear, and do bear, on our every-day life, on our daily conflict with sin and temptation; while those other truths of the eternal relation of the Son to the Father, for which Athanasius strove, for which he was contented to be an exile and a fugitive, a dweller in caves and in wildernesses, to brave the extremest wrath of the world's mightiest potentate—these, with others which like them seem to lie remote from our own immediate need, awaken no lively sympathy in our hearts. We confess their importance; we should strive, it may be most earnestly, against those who should deliberately seek to rob us of them; we should probably then understand that they were the strong substructures which, however out of sight, did yet support the fabric of our faith, that would be weak and tottering without them; but they are not now in any sense dear and near to us, like those doctrines of grace, for which Augustine witnessed, or of justification, from which Luther shook the dust of ages three centuries ago. Yet surely it was not for nothing that in the early Church the word "theology," with more special reference to its derivation, was restricted to that portion of what *we* should call theology, which had to do with God himself, with the ever-blessed Trinity, or with the Son in his divine nature; while by other words, as for instance the "economy," men were used to designate the appearance of the Son of God in time, his life and walk in the flesh, his directly redemptive work. Those who employed this language did feel, and rightly, that in God the root of all theology lay; that he was the subject-matter of it, and consciously or unconsciously they expressed this conviction by the limitation which they assigned to the word.

And the dangers which beset us when we at all forget this, are indeed neither few nor insignificant. Theology, when it limits itself to the immediately practical and useful, dismissing everything which it does not esteem such, will not long retain even that practical and useful to which it has been willing to sacrifice everything besides. Its pastures will lose their greenness soon, its lower levels will become dry and parched and barren, if they be not fed and refreshed from the upper springs. Its conversation must be habitually in heaven, if it shall really have anything which is worth the telling upon earth. It is a Jacob's ladder, but angels must *de*scend upon it, no less than *a*scend. If there be none descending, there will in a little while be none to ascend. In it we must have the story, not *merely* of man's upward striving to God; indeed, not of this at all, except as the result of God's downward looking upon men. It is not the record of a religious sentiment in man, a pathology of the human soul under certain of its higher aspects, but a record of a divine revelation from God, of what he has announced to men of his own being. In the fact that we are sometimes forgetting this, that there is so much about man, and so little about God in our modern theology, lies in great part the secret of its weakness; of the feeble hold which it has upon numbers who would gladly learn what God has declared of himself; but who care much less for any secondary notices as to the exact manner in which this message has affected others; and least of all for what others have thought and speculated about him.

If we would be delivered from these dangers, and re-assert for that which is the queen-science of all, her rightful dominion over the hearts and spirits of men, we must learn to fall back more on those transcendent truths of which the prologue of St. John is full—to meditate on them more fully and more frequently—to bring them into greater prominence for ourselves and for others—to believe that it was not for nothing that this Scripture, or the first chapter of Colossians, was written. We must learn to connect our Lord's manifestation in the flesh, not indeed less with all which followed it, his death, his resurrection, his ascension, his glorified sitting at the right hand of the Majesty on high; but to connect it more with that which preceded, his eternal generation, the glory which he had with the Father before the world was, the creation of all worlds by him, and above all, of man, not merely by him, but *in* him, and *for* him, and *to* him; and this so really, that even had there been no

Fall, an Incarnation, a coming forth on his part, as at once the root and perfect flower of our nature, would probably not the less have been.

It behoves us, indeed, to speak with hesitation and modesty on a matter like this. Had there been no Fall, the conditions under which that transcendent manifestation of love and of honor done to man must have taken place, would of course have been infinitely different from those under which the Eternal Son did actually exchange the form of God for the form of a servant, and become obedient unto death, even the death of the cross. Those conditions, more glorious seemingly, would have been less glorious in reality, for they would have lacked the glory of suffering, the unfathomable wonder of that infinite self-denial which stooped to the fallen and the guilty, and shared the miseries of the one and the penalties of the other. But the thing itself, we may reverently believe, would not the less have been. They only re-affirm what has been the conviction of many theologians in all times, who are persuaded that the headship of the race of man would have pertained to him not the less, to whom all headship of men or of angels rightly appertains; all things in heaven and in earth being recapitulated in him; since only in this recapitulation could the race of Adam have attained the end of its creation, the place among the families of God, for which from the first it was designed.

In this view, the taking on Himself of our flesh by the Eternal Word was no makeshift, to meet a mighty, yet still a particular emergent, need; a need which, conceding the liberty of man's will and that it was possible for him to have continued in his first state of obedience, might never have occurred. It was not a mere result and reparation of the Fall, such an act as, except for that, would never have been; but lay bedded at a far deeper depth in the counsels of God for the glory of his Son, and the exaltation of that race formed in his image and his likeness. For against those who regard the Incarnation as an arbitrary, or as merely an historic event, and not an ideal one as well, we may well urge this weighty consideration, that the Son of God did not in and after his ascension strip off this human nature again; he did not regard his humanity as a robe, to be worn for awhile, and then laid aside; the convenient form of his manifestation, so long as he was conversing with men upon earth, but the fitness of which had with that conversation passed away. So far from this, we know on the contrary that he assumed our nature for ever, married it to himself, glorified it with his own glory, carried it as the form of his eternal subsistence into the world of angels, before the presence of his Father. Had there been anything accidental here, had the assumption of our nature been an afterthought (I speak as a man), this marriage of the Son of God with that nature could scarcely be conceived. He could hardly have so taken it—taken it, that is, for ever—unless it had possessed an ideal as well as an historic fitness; unless pre-established harmonies had existed, such harmonies as only a divine intention could have brought about between the one and the other.

What those pre-established harmonies were the words of the heathen poet, but words adopted and made his own by the Christian Apostle, declare—" For we are all his offspring;" words, be it remembered, not addressed to the regenerate, and on the ground of their regeneration, but addressed by St. Paul to his heathen listeners at Athens. Children of this world, children of wrath, as all or nearly all of those listeners may well have been when he addressed them, he yet did not fear to bring them back to their divine original, to remind them of the ideal heights and primeval destinies of man—all forfeited in Adam, and now won back and recovered in Christ; but which yet had been only recoverable, because they were a portion of man's original inheritance; because in the fact that man was God's offspring, or God's race, the possibility lay that One should come forth from God, he too God's Son from eternity, fulfilling this name to the uttermost; who should place his shoulders under the mighty ruin of our race, should arrest its fall, and so vindicate his right to exclaim, "The earth and its inhabiters are dissolved. I bear up the pillars thereof."

It seems to me, therefore, that in discoursing of the Word made flesh, we may fitly, as regards the redeemed, carry back our thoughts to that creation of man in God's image and likeness, which alone rendered an Incarnation possible. We may fitly also, as respects the Redeemer, declare that we regard that but as one step, the last indeed, and most glorious one, of his manifestation, that he who so manifested himself then, had been manifesting himself from the beginning of the world; and not of our world only; for the Apostle speaks of another and a higher world in these words, "When he bringeth in the First Begotten into the world he saith, And let all the angels of God worship him." But yet in our world also we may affirm that he had been manifesting himself long before, patriarch and prophet walking in his light, encountering him, as he, the Angel of the Covenant, the Captain of the Lord's Host, preluded his Incarnation by transient assumptions of a human form. Yea, every spark of higher life which was not trodden out in heathendom, we have a right, resting on this Scripture, to declare that it was he who kept it alive, that this light shining in men's darkness was *his* light, his unextinguished and inextinguishable witness in the hearts and consciences of men.

When, however, the light shining in the darkness proved ever more unable to scatter it, for "the darkness comprehended it not," then there followed another step in the manifestation of the Eternal Word. He who was the divine ground of man's being, himself became man: "the Word was made flesh, and dwelt among us (and we beheld his glory, the glory as of the only begotten of the Father), full of grace and truth."—"We beheld," exclaims the Apostle, "his glory." And what was the glory which he beheld? The fullness of his grace and truth. Not in the fullness of his power, not in the mighty works which he wrought, or which were wrought on him, not in signs and miracles and wonders, not in any of these did the Apostle detect "the glory as of the only begotten of the Father;" but in this, that he went up and down the world with words of truth, and gracious deeds of healing; that he preached the Gospel to the poor, that he stooped to every need, had a heart for every wo. In these things shone out the glory which the beloved disciple saw.

Oh, brethren, what potent medicine is here for the pride and swellings of our souls! We have in *his* life of whom St. John is speaking the human when it is most godlike; nay, rather, we have here man in his actual identity with God. Surely this must be man, as he most ought to be; and oh! how unlike he proves to that dream of human greatness which we sometimes would fain realize for ourselves, which we are ready to wonder after when realized in others. What a witness is here borne against that worship of force—moral or immoral, it matters little—to which some would so earnestly invite us, which is only too welcome to our selves; as though strength, if only it be strong enough, contained ever an apology for itself, justified and redeemed its own excesses, became a law to itself, and might own no other law; the ten commandments, with their "Love God," and "Love your neighbor," having been never meant for the leading spirits of the world—so that, to hear some speak, we might suppose that holiness and righteousness are only one of the many ways in which men are free to develop themselves and their own inward life; while if their taste and impulses are in another direction, they are equally free to choose that other. But here at length is the divine idea of humanity; the one man, about whom, if we believe anything, we must believe that his life is normal and regulative for the lives of all other men; and that life how different from, and how far rebuking, those lives of "the men of the earth," the proud and strong, for whom our admiration is demanded.

And then, as another fruit of the Incarnation, it not merely delivers us from false standards of glory and of greatness, giving us for these the true, but, much more than this, supplies us with a deliverance from the same disease of our spirits, when it has reached a far higher intensity. We have thus a man whom men may worship, and yet not be guilty of idolatry; whom they are bound to worship, for he is also the Son of God, if they would not be guilty of impiety. Herein is deliverance from the last and subtlest form of all idolatry, the deification and worship of man, and, worst of all, of him in all which constitutes his shame no less than his glory. The race of mankind, growing intellectually to man's estate, may outlive and leave far behind every other form of false worship. It may no longer fill a profaned pantheon with birds and beasts and creeping things. The beneficent powers of nature may no longer attract, nor the blind forces of nature extort, its homage; hero and demigod may pertain to creeds outworn and a long-vanished past; but there is an idol-worship which remains still behind, and from which there is no deliverance, except in him in whom alone is deliverance from all idolatry, and who alone satisfies the yearnings out of which it springs. "God is man," or "Man is God"— we must choose between these two statements, and accept the tremendous consequences of our choice. A time in the development of the history of our race arrives, when these are the only alternatives for every man. And if we are willing to believe St. Paul and St. John, be sure, brethren, that the question in the end will present itself to every man in a very palpable form, and one from which there shall be no escape, but that he must answer it one way or the other. Will he accept the God-man, him who was God from everlasting before he was made man; or in lieu of him, a man-god, a man that has lifted up himself, and been lifted up by the consent of his fellows, to this blasphemous height?

Nor is it Scripture alone which declares this: he must be blind indeed to the moral signs of the times, who can not perceive this mystery of iniquity, the last and the crowning one, already working; this world-wide conspiracy, the same of which David spake in the second Psalm, spreading through an apostate Christendom which is ripening more and more for an open revolt from its Lord. "Man is God," this is the new Gospel, which is seeking to supplant the old, or "God is man." It needs hardly be observed that this new gospel is indeed atheism, and that veiled under thinnest disguise. For "Man is God," what after all does it amount to but this—"Man is man"? for they who so speak, having in this very utterance evidently renounced a belief in God, in a Being, that is greater, better, holier, wiser, than man, have no right to retain and juggle with a name which belongs to another and a higher range of things than any which they would acknowledge, to deck themselves with its spoils, and by aid of these to cover and conceal their own miserable poverty; crouching, like some barbarous horde, beneath the ruins of temples and palaces which they themselves have destroyed.

But leaving this, which is but by the way, the time will assuredly arrive when every man will have to choose for the one or the other. So was it at the first founding of the Church, when martyr and confessor took their side, braving all and enduring all, rather than that they would give to any other man the honor and the worship which was rightfully their Lord's. So shall it be once more, amid fiercer fires and yet sharper trials, when the Church is passing through the final agony, "the great tribulation," which shall precede its entrance into glory. What the Godman is, in meekness, in patience, in love, in holiness, this the history of Jesus of Nazareth abundantly declares. Nor are we left in total ignorance of what the man-god will prove. We need but to study him in the completest manifestation which he has yet assumed, I mean, of course, in the deified emperors of Rome, a Tiberius, a Nero, or a Domitian, and we may a little guess the moral lineaments which he will wear. What altogether he will be, it is reserved for the final Antichrist, in his yet more complete opposition to all which is divine, in the final apotheosis of man, to declare; when he, being indeed incarnate sin, shall "as God sit in the temple of God, showing himself that he is God," and being accepted and worshipped as such by all save the little company (and they will be a little one then), who shall recognise in Jesus of Nazareth the only begotten of the Father, and who in the strength of this confession, "I believe in Jesus Christ, the Son of God," shall overcome at last by the blood of the Lamb, issuing triumphantly from those fires in which they shall have been purified and made white and tried. To this decision, to this solemn consummation, the world's moral history, "the times of the Gentiles," are travelling, and by ever faster strides.

But we must conclude, and we will do it with one observation more. The Apostle who said, "We beheld his glory, the glory as of the only begotten of the Father," and who seemed to lay, and no doubt did lay, such stress on this beholding, is the same who alone among the Evangelists reports those words of his Lord, "Because thou hast seen me, Thomas, thou hast believed; blessed are they that have not seen, and yet have believed." This is the abiding blessedness, the blessedness which is equally for all. With spiritual eyes (and after all it was only with these that the beloved Apostle himself beheld the glory of his Lord; without these he might have seen *him*, as so many others did, yet never seen his glory)—with spiritual eyes we too may "behold the glory as of the only begotten, full of grace and truth." Beholding him, we may be transformed into his image and likeness; worshipping him, we may be delivered from every false worship; believing on him, we may receive power to become all which "sons of God," that name which we have borne from our baptisms, involves.

# SERMON II.

## CHRIST THE LAMB OF GOD.

# SERMON II.

## CHRIST THE LAMB OF GOD.

### John i. 29.

*The next day John seeth Jesus coming unto him, and saith, Behold the Lamb of God, which taketh away the sin of the world.*

It has been sometimes asked and debated, to which of the lambs of sacrifice, ordained in the Old Testament, did the Baptist here refer; with which did he liken that immaculate Lamb, who, being without spot and stain, should take away our spots and stains, and bear the collective sin of the world. Did St. John allude to the daily lamb of the morning and evening sacrifice?—or was it to the lamb of the passover, commemorating the old deliverance from Egypt?—or was it to some other of the many lambs which were prescribed in the law of Moses, as a portion of the ritual of sacrifice appointed there? The question is surely a superfluous one. The reference is not special, but comprehensive. It is to none of these in particular, being indeed to them all. They severally set forth in type and in figure some part of that which He fulfilled in substance and in full; in him, not now a lamb of men, but the Lamb of God, being at length fulfilled to the uttermost the significant word of Abraham, "God will provide himself a lamb."

The disciples of John understand the intention with which he thus designated Jesus unto them; they understand it, if not at the first designation, yet at the second; and as the Evangelist tells us (he probably was himself one of the two disciples, Andrew being the other), they "heard him speak, and they followed Jesus." They quitted one master, and joined themselves to another. There was a drawing, attractive power in that word about the Lamb, the taker away of the world's sin, which no other word possessed or could possess. At a later day, Christ himself declared, " I, if I be lifted up, will draw all men unto me." Already this potent drawing had begun. Set between two magnets, the disciples showed at once which was the mightier of the two. John indeed had met many needs of men's spirits—their need of repentance, of confession of sin, of amendment of life; but there were other needs which he could not meet. The spirit of man cries out for something deeper even than these, something which shall reach farther back; which shall not be clogged with sinful infirmities, as his own repentance even at the very best must be. Men cry for some work to rest upon, which shall not be *their* work, and thus underlying the weaknesses of everything human, but which shall be God's; perfect, complete, to which nothing need be added, from which nothing can be taken away. They feel that behind and beyond their repentance, even though that repentance be wrought by the Spirit of God, there must be something which God has not so much wrought *in* them, as *for* them; and that on this they must rest, if they are to find abiding peace for the soul; a rock to flee to, which is higher than they; higher than their repentance, than their faith, than their obedience, even than their new life in the Spirit. Now this Rock is Christ; and John pointed to this Rock, and the two at once understood him. They had longed after amendment of life, and John had helped them thus far; but they yearned for more than this, for atonement, propitiation, ransom, a conscience purged from dead works by the blood of sprinkling, and John could not help them here; except indeed by directing them to Jesus, as in these memorable words he did, "Behold the Lamb of God, which taketh away the sin of the world."

It is impossible to estimate too highly the significance of these words, or the place which, in a true scheme of Christian doctrine, they must assume. As the Church understands them, they set forth our Lord in his central function and office, as the one perfect sacrifice, "the Lamb of God:" they set forth the effectual operation of his sacrifice of himself, as a bearing, and a bearing away, of the world's sin. They may therefore fitly constitute our starting-point from which to consider what the Church's doctrine of the atonement, or of the sacrifice of the death of Christ, and of the consequences which follow thereupon, may be; and this, with especial reference to objections brought against this doctrine, as failing to commend itself to the conscience, as indeed outraging that sense of right, that revelation anterior to all other revelations, which God has planted in the heart; as a doctrine therefore, which, however it may seem to be in Scripture, however a superficial interpretation of certain passages may favor this impression, it is impossible can be truly there.

The gravity of the matter thus brought to issue none can deny, nor yet the very serious and far-reaching consequences which must follow, if, while the word "sacrifice" should indeed be left us, all wherein the essence of sacrifice consisted, as mainly its *vicarious* and *satisfactory* character, were to be exploded from the New Testament. One of the first of these consequences would be a loosening, that I say not a dissolution, of the bonds between the Old Testament and the New. There can be no question that in the Old, the doctrine of sacrifice, of the vicarious suffering of one for another, of satisfaction resulting thereupon, everywhere prevails. If there is nothing of this in the New, if this is Jewish only and not Christian as well, if Christ, for instance, is only the Lamb of God because of his innocence and purity, and not because of his sacrificial death, if he takes away the sin of the world only in the way of summoning and enabling men to leave off their sins, all bonds between the New Testament and at least the Levitical sacrifices of the Old are broken. These last point to nothing. They are a huge husk without a kernel; types without their antetype; shadows, but not "shadows of the true," and thus with no substance following; a promise without performance; an elaborate and enormous machinery for the effecting of nothing.

That which hitherto has ennobled those sacrifices in our eyes, was the truth which they foreshowed. Let them have foreshowed nothing of the kind, and they sink down at once to a level with the heathen sacrifices; nay, not merely to a level with those, as those have hitherto been regarded by us, but they drag down to a far lower depth the heathen and themselves together. Hitherto the heathen sacrifices, hideous distortions of the true as they so often were, yet were not without a certain terrible grandeur of their own. A ray of the glory of Calvary fell upon them, and, dark as they remained, yet did not leave them all dark. They were blind feelings after the cross of Christ, passionate outcries for it; they were lies indeed, yet lies which cried after the truth. But take from Christ's cross its character of an altar, and from his death its character of a sacrifice, and at once the Levitical sacrifices no longer remain as shadows of the true, and the heathen cease to be remote resemblances of the same. Let the doctrine of Christ's death as being a vicarious atonement and satisfaction be dismissed from the New Testament, on the ground of its contradiction to the righteous moral instincts of humanity, and it is impossible consistently to maintain the divine character of large portions of the Old.

But let us a little consider what the objections are, which are now being made to the Church's doctrine of the atonement, and what the answers which they seem to demand. And first in regard to this discussion it may be generally observed, that it is *not* sufficient to reply to these objections out of Scripture; the very argument of the objectors being, that the meaning we attach to our Scripture proofs can not be the right one, revolting, as it does, that sense of righteousness and justice which is God's gift to men anterior to all other gifts, that earliest revelation of himself which no later one can ever gainsay or set aside, but into harmony with which each later must be brought. We must seek our arguments elsewhere. We must endeavor first to show, and, confined within the narrow bounds of a single discourse, I shall limit myself to this — how that truth which we affirm, does not offend, but indeed commends itself to, the moral sense; by manifestation of the truth commending ourselves and it to the consciences of men.

The objection, then, as I take it, to Christ's *vicarious* offering — for I will first deal with this — to the assertion that he died not merely for the good of, but in the room and in the stead of, others, tasted death *for* them, commonly assumes this form. Must not righteousness, it is said, be the law of all God's dealings? Most of all, must we not expect to find consistent with highest righteousness that which is the most solemn and awful dealing of God with his creatures? But how is it agreeable with this, how can it be called just, nay, how can it be acquitted of extremest injustice, to lay on one man the penalties of others, so that he pays the things which he never took, so that they sin and he is punished, on him being laid the iniquities of them all? What have we here, an adversary will insist, but in the awfullest sphere of all, and in matters the most tremendous, the same injustice which, even in least things, provokes our indignation;

as, for instance, when some playfellow of a young prince is constituted, as we may sometimes have read of, to suffer the consequences of *his* idleness; so that one neglects his tasks, and another is chastised; one plays the truant, and another bears the smart?

But the case is not in point; and, since it has been started, it might be worth our while to make it in point, and then to consider whether it presents itself in any aspect so monstrous and absurd. To make it in point, the parts which the several persons sustain must, in the first place, be reversed. It must be that the young prince suffers for his humbler truant companions, not one of them for him; it must be that he does it, not of compulsion or constraint, but of his own free will; it must be that only such an act as this would overcome their perversity and idleness; that he offers himself to this correction, knowing that nothing else would overcome it, and that this would be effectual to do so. A submission with this knowledge to the punishment of their faults and negligences and shortcomings might be strange, even as all acts of condescending self-offering love are strange in a world of selfishness and pride; but surely there would be nothing in it either monstrous or ridiculous.

And exactly in the same way, when we hear it urged, How can it be righteous to lay on one man the penalties of others? surely we must feel that the question, to be effectually answered, needs only to be more accurately put; that the form which it ought to assume is this, How can it be righteous for one man *to take upon himself* the penalties of others? and none who remember the "Lo! I come" of the Saviour, the willing sacrifice of our Issac, prefigured by his who climbed so meekly in his father's company the hill of Moriah—none, I say, who remember this, will deny our right to make this change; while surely the whole aspect of the question is now by this little change altered altogether. For how many an act of heroic self-sacrifice, which it would be most unrighteous for others to demand from, or to force on, one reluctant, which indeed would cease to be heroism or sacrifice at all, unless wholly self-imposed, is yet most glorious when one has freely offered himself thereunto; is only *not* righteous, because it is so much better than righteous, because it moves in that higher region where law is no more known, but only known no more because it has been transfigured into love. Wherein else is the chief glory of history but in those deeds of self-devotion, of heroic self-offering, which, like trumpet-tones sounding from the depths of the past, rouse us, at least for a while, from the selfish dream of life to a nobler existence; and of which if the mention has become trite and common now, it has only become so because the grandeur of them has caused them to be evermore in the hearts and on the lips of men. Vicarious suffering, it is strange to hear the mighty uproar which is made about it; when indeed in lower forms—not low in themselves, though low as compared with the highest—it is everywhere, where love is at all. For indeed is not this, one freely taking on himself the consequences of other's faults, and thus averting from those others at least in part the penalties of the same, building what others have thrown down, gathering what others have scattered bearing the burdens which others have wrapped together, healing the wounds which others have inflicted, paying the things which he never took, smarting for sins which he never committed; is not this, I say, the law and the condition of all highest nobleness in the world?—is it not that which God is continually demanding of his elect, they approving themselves his elect, as they do not shrink from this demand, as they freely own themselves the debtors of love to the last penny of the requirements which it makes? And if these things are so, shall we question the right of God himself to display this nobleness which he demands of his creatures? Shall we wish to rob him of the opportunity, or think to honor him who is highest love, by denying him the right, to display it?

But the sufferings and death of Christ were not merely vicarious; they were also satisfactory; and thus atoning or setting *at one*, bringing together the Holy and the unholy, who could not have been reconciled in any other way. When we speak thus, we are sometimes taunted at the outset with the fact that the word "satisfaction," as applied to the death of Christ and its results, nowhere occurs in Scripture; so belongs to the later Latin theology (Anselm being the first to employ it), that the Greek theology does not so much as possess the word —I mean of course any Greek equivalent for it. This is true; but though the word "satisfaction" is not in Scripture, the thing is everywhere there, and we are contending not about words, but things; the idea of it is inherent in ransom, in redemption, in propitiation, in scriptural words and phrases and images out of number; and just as in the Arian controversy, the Church had a perfect right to the "homo-ousion," careless whether the *word* were in Scripture or no, so here to "satisfaction," seeing that this best expresses and sums up the truth which in this matter she holds.

But, not to tarry longer with this objection at the threshold, how, it is further urged, could God be well pleased with the sufferings of the innocent and the holy? What "satisfaction," since we will have this word, could he find in these? Here, as so often, the faith of the Church is first caricatured, that so it may be more easily brought into question. Could God have pleasure in the sufferings of the innocent and the holy, and that innocent and holy his own Son? Assuredly not; but he could have pleasure, nay, according to the moral necessities of his own being, he must have pleasure, yea, the highest joy, satisfaction, and delight, in the love, the patience, the obedience, which those sufferings gave him the opportunity of displaying, which but for those he could never have displayed; above all he must have rejoiced in these as manifested in his own Son For even we ourselves, when we read in story of those who for the love of their fellows have made their lives one long patient martyrdom, or who, witnessing for the truth, have been borne from earth in the fire-chariot of some shorter but sharper agony, do we not feel that we have a right to rejoice in these martyrs of truth and love, yea, in the very pains and sufferings which they endured? that only as the nerves of our own moral being are weak and unstrung, only as we have become incapable not merely of doing, but even of appreciating, what is noble and great, do we grudge them those pains, do we wish for them one of these to have been less; seeing that these were the conditions of their greatness, that without which it could never have been shown, without which it might never have existed?

Even the heathen moralist could say of God in his dealings with good men, "*fortiter* amat;" there is no weakness in his love; it is love according to which he does not spare his own, but thrusts them forth to labor and difficulty and pains, in which alone they can be perfected; even as the same heathe could affirm that God had joy in nobly suffering men; not, of course, for the sufferings' sake, but for the virtues which were manifested therein. And should not the

God and Father of our Lord Jesus Christ have pleasure in the faith, the love, the obedience of his Son? Yea, it was a joy such as only the mind and heart of God could contain, that in his Son this perfect pattern of self-forgetting, self-offering love was displayed. We do not shrink from accepting in the simplest sense the assertion of the Apostle, that Christ, giving himself for us on the Cross, became therein and thereby "a sacrifice of a sweet-smelling savor" unto God; that he was well pleased therewith, and said at length what he would never else have said, "I have found a ransom."

Christ satisfied herein—not the divine anger—but the divine craving and yearning after a perfect holiness, righteousness, and obedience in man, God's chosen creature, the first-fruits of his creatures; which craving no man had satisfied, but all had disappointed, before. There had been a flaw in every other man's escutcheon; every other, instead of repairing the breach which Adam had made, had himself left that breach wider than he found it. But here at length was one, a son of man, yet fairer than all the children of men, one on whom the Father's love could rest with a perfect complacency, in regard of whom he could declare, "This is my beloved Son, in whom I am well pleased," in whom he had pleasure without stint and without drawback. And that life of his, the long self-offering of that life of love was crowned, consummated, and perfected, by the sacrifice of his death, wherein he satisfied to the uttermost every demand which God could make on him, and satisfied for all the demands which God had made upon all the other children of men, and which they had not satisfied for themselves.

But if the question is here asked, How could one man satisfy for many? how by one man's obedience could many be made righteous? the answer is not far to seek. The transcendent worth of that obedience which Christ rendered, of that oblation which he offered, the power which it possessed of countervailing and counterbalancing a world's sin, lay in this, that he who offered these, while he bore a human nature, and wrought human acts, was a Divine person; not indeed God alone, for as such he would never have been in the condition to offer; nor man alone, for then the worth of his offering could never have reached so far; but that he was God and man in one person indissolubly united, and in this person performing all those acts, man that he might obey and suffer and die, God that he might add to every act of his obedience, his suffering, his death, an immeasurable worth, steeping in the glory of his divine personality all of human that he wrought. Christ was able so summarily to pay our debt, because he had another and a higher coin in which to pay it than that in which it was contracted. It was contracted in the currency of earth; he paid it in the currency of heaven. Nor was it, as some among the schoolmen of the Middle Ages taught, that God arbitrarily ascribed and imputed to Christ's obedience unto death a value which made it equal to the needs and sins of the world, such a value as it would not have had but for this imputation. We affirm rather with the deeper theologians of those and of all times, who crave to deal with realities, not with ascriptions and imputations, that his offering had in itself this intrinsic value, that there was no ascription to it, as of God's mere pleasure, of a value which it did not in itself possess; for then the same might have been imputed to the work of an angel or of a saint; the whole exclusive fitness of the Son of God undertaking the work would then pass away; and another might have made up the breach as well as he. We affirm rather that what the Son of God claimed in behalf of that race whereof he had become the representative and the Head, he claimed as of right—although, indeed, that right was one which the Father as joyfully conceded as the Son demanded. Without a satisfaction such as this the eternal interests of that righteousness whereof God is the upholder in his own moral universe would not have permitted him to be, as he now is, the passer-by of transgression, the justifier and accepter of the ungodly.

Such, my brethren, is the Church's faith in respect of the atonement. That atonement is not, as some would persuade us, a one-sided act; it looks not one way only, but two; having a face with which it looks toward God, as well as one with which it looks toward man. It is no mere reconciling of man to God, as though its object were to remove the distrust, to kill the enmity in man's heart, to persuade him to throw down his arms, and yield himself the vanquished of eternal love. It is most truly this, but it is much more than this. It is a reconciling not merely of man to God, but of God to man; whose love could not have gone forth upon the children of men in its highest forms, in those of forgiveness, acceptance, renewal, if this had not found place. Think not then, my brethren, of Christ the peace *maker*, as though he came only to *announce* peace; to say to the doubting and distrustful children of men, "Why will ye remain at such a miserable and guilty distance from your heavenly Father, when his arms are stretched out to receive you, when he is only waiting to enfold you within them?" No doubt Christ did come bringing this message, did proclaim that those arms were open, tnat heavenly Father waiting to be gracious, but he only brought this inasmuch as he *made* the peace which he announced. "Having *made* peace (εἰρηνοποιήσας) by the blood of his Cross," "he entered into the holiest of all, having obtained (or, having himself *found*, εὑράμενος) eternal redemption for us." In him and through him, through the sacrifice of death, the disturbed, and in part suspended relations between God and his sinful creatures, were reconstituted anew; his blood being shed to cleanse men from their sins, and not to teach them that those sins needed no cleansing, and could be forgiven without one.

And will any faith which is short of this faith satisfy the deepest needs and cravings of your souls? You may struggle against it with your understandings; though, I think, very needlessly; for it seems to me to approve itself to the reason and the conscience, quite as much as to

demand acceptance of our faith; but you will
crave it with your inmost spirits. There are
times when, perhaps, nothing short of this will
save you from a hopeless despair. Let me imagine, for example, one, who with many capaci-
ties for a nobler and purer life, and many calls
thereunto, has yet suffered himself to be entan-
gled in youthful lusts, has stained himself with
these; and then after a while awakens, or rather
is awakened by the good Spirit of God, to ask
himself, What have I done? How fares it with
him at the retrospect then, when he, not wholly
laid waste in spirit, is made to possess (oh, fearful possession!) the sins of his youth? Like a
stricken deer, though none but himself may be
conscious of his wound, he wanders away from
his fellows; or if with them, he is alone among
them, for he is brooding still and ever on the
awful mystery of evil which he now too nearly
knows. And now too all purity, the fearful innocence of children, the holy love of sister and
of mother, and the love which he had once
dreamed of as better even than these, with all

which is supremely fair in nature or in art, comes to him with a shock of pain, is fraught with an infinite sadness; for it wakens up in him by contrast a livelier sense of what he is, and what, as it seems, he must for ever. be; it reminds him of a Paradise for ever lost, the angel of God's anger guarding with a fiery sword its entrance against him. He tries by a thousand devices to still, or at least to deaden, the undying pain of his spirit. What is this word sin, that it should torment him so? He will tear away the conscience of it, this poisonous shirt of Nessus, eating into his soul, which in a heedless moment he has put on. But no; he can tear away his own flesh, but he can not tear away that. Go where he may, he still carries with him the barbed shaft which has pierced him; "hæret lateri letalis arundo." The arrow which drinks up his spirit, there is no sovereign dittany which will cause it to drop from his side—none, that is, which grows on earth; but there is, which grows in heaven, and in the Church of Christ, the heavenly enclosure here. And you too, if such a one be among us, may find your peace, you will find it, when you learn to look by faith on him, "the Lamb of God, that taketh away the sin of the world." You will carry, it may be, the scars of those wounds which you have inflicted upon yourself to your grave; but the wounds themselves he can heal them, and heal them altogether. He can give you back the years which the cankerworm has eaten, the peace which your sin had chased away, and, as it seemed to you, for ever. He can do so and will. "Purge me with hyssop, and I shall be clean, wash me, and I shall be whiter than snow"—this will be then your prayer, and this your prayer will be fulfilled. The blood of sprinkling will purge, and you will feel yourself clean. Your sin will no longer be yourself; you will be able to look at it as separated from you, as laid upon another, upon One so strong that he did but for a moment stagger under the weight of a world's sin, and then so bore, that bearing he has borne it away for ever.

# SERMON III.

## CHRIST THE LIGHT OF THE WORLD.

# SERMON III.

## CHRIST THE LIGHT OF THE WORLD.

John viii. 12.

Then spake Jesus unto them again, saying, I am the Light of the world; he that followeth me shall not walk in darkness, but shall have the light of life.

An attentive and thoughtful student of the Gospel of St. John will scarcely have failed to observe the manner in which almost everything there seems to revolve round certain leading antitheses — as few as they are comprehensive, as simple as they are sublime. The spirit and the flesh, truth and falsehood, life and death, or, as here, light and darkness, these recur continually; the burden of the highest and deepest things of the kingdom of God, and of that other kingdom opposed to his kingdom, is laid upon them; and they answer all purposes, and meet every need. It is the very character of genius even in things earthly and uninspired, that with simplest implements and fewest materials it brings about the mightiest and most marvellous results. Exactly so is it here, in a yet higher sphere; in that not of human genius, but of divine inspiration. The Lord himself, and the Evangelist who has learned not merely to record, but to think and speak his Lord's language, move among these few, but at the same time vast and comprehensive contrasts, and by their aid set forth to us the life *in* God, which is life, and the life *out* of God, which is death; all that is to be sought, and all that is to be shunned; they set forth this as no accumulation of words and images, no pomp of rhetoric could ever have availed to do it.

There are those to whom the diction of the Evangelist in its extreme simplicity, the language of the Lord himself, as he utters himself in this fourth Gospel, will seem poor at a first acquaintance with it; but just as St. Paul declared " the foolishness of God is wiser than men," so, with the example of his bold utterance before us, we also may be bold to say, " the poverty of God is richer than men," than all the treasures of their eloquence, than all the wealth of their words; and never does a conviction of this come home to us with greater force than when we study as we ought the Gospel and Epistles of St. John. How simple, for example, and yet how far-reaching the words before us: " I am the Light of the world; he that followeth me shall not walk in darkness, but shall have the light of life." They move in a sphere of imagery the most obvious, light and darkness being, so to speak, primary moral symbols, symbols respectively of knowledge and of ignorance in the intellectual world, of good and evil in the ethical. I suppose that no nation has ever existed on the earth which has shifted and reversed the significance of these symbols; for whom light has represented ignorance and evil, or darkness knowledge and good; and it is quite inconceivable that such a reversing of their significance should ever suggest itself to any. The symbolism is anterior to, and independent of, all agreement; it admits of no discussion; it is incapable of any change; being rooted in those mysterious correspondencies between the natural and moral world, which bear testimony at once to their own inherent and unchangeable fitness. Angels are and ever will be regarded by us as clothed with light, in shining robes; yea, God himself will clothe himself for all with light as with a garment, will dwell in light inaccessible, will be the light as the life of men; while the kingdom of evil will be contemplated evermore as a kingdom of darkness, and evil works as deeds of darkness; even as an element in the glory of the heavenly Jerusalem has been set forth to us under these words: "There was no night there."

But to consider these words more nearly, I would entreat you to observe, my brethren, how the Lord assumes in them, as in so many other of his words, as indeed more or less distinctly in all his words, a central position in respect of the whole family of mankind; so that all men stand in a relation to him in which they do not stand to one other, or to any child of man except only to himself. He presents himself, not as other men are, a point, it may be an important one, but still a point, in the vast circumference of humanity. He is rather the centre *to* which the lines from every other point converge; *from* which they diffuse themselves again. And in respect of this, how different is Christ's self-assertion, from the self-negation of every other good and holy man. Every other, in proportion as he is a good man and true, rejoices to make himself nothing, to divest himself of every glory and of every claim. The Baptist was great (we have an angel's word for it), but when his countrymen asked him, " Who art thou? what sayest thou of thyself?" the utmost he would claim was, to be " a voice crying in the wilderness;" he was, he proclaimed, of the earth, and being earthly, spake of the earth, and seemed to rejoice in words of self-disparagement.

But while he and every other godly man thus abdicates every claim, puts back, at least before

God, the honor which others would thrust upon him, while every other thus makes himself nothing, Christ, on the contrary, makes himself everything. He puts himself, I will not say into the foremost rank, for that would ill express the fact, but into a rank quite by himself. And yet he who did so, was, as we know, the meek and the lowly one, was clothed with humility, came seeking not his own glory, but the glory of his Father; while for all this no words are too large, no statements too magnificent, for him to utter in respect of himself. All the weary and heavy laden in this vast wilderness of wo are to come to him; he has rest and refreshment for them all. He predominates over all human relations, the nearest and the holiest; to love father or mother better than him, is not to be worthy of him. He is the Bread of God, which men may eat of and not die—the Resurrection and the Life—the Way, the Truth, and the Life—the True Vine—or, as here, the Light of the world.

Surely this fact, this contrast between Christ's language about himself, and other good men's language about themselves, may well give rise to profound meditations; the conclusions which we may deduce from it are of infinite importance. How many heresies which have torn the Church it ought to have rendered for ever impossible. For how impossible is it to reconcile these declarations of the Lord about himself with any other view of the dignity of his person save that which the Catholic Church in all ages has held. He is either that which the Church teaches him to be—or that which we may well decline to utter in an assembly of Christian men. There is no other alternative. If these declarations which Christ makes about himself are true, then all temporizing middle positions, Arian, and Unitarian, are such as it is impossible to maintain. Men can not rest in them for long; but must either rise higher, that is, to the faith of the Church in respect of her Lord; or else sink lower, and renounce the Lord of glory as a deceiver, or a deceived. For as many as accept the Evangelists' record of our Lord's words as perfectly representing what he did utter, unmodified, uncolored by prejudices and prepossessions of the relater, every other position but one of these, is one merely of transition, is one logically untenable, and is sooner or later discovered to be so, and forsaken.

A man might claim, for instance, to be *a* light, as John " was a burning and a shining light;" but what man to be *the* light? Or he might claim to be the light of some single age or some single people, though in a very secondary and subordinate sense ; but to be " the light of the world," who but the Creator of the world could, without intolerable presumption, such as would convict him to be not light at all, but darkness, claim to be this? Others indeed, who had caught some scattered rays of his brightness before he rose visibly above the horizon, had been the light of this land or of that; of this age or the other. But, as was said, in how secondary and subordinate a sense! They brought *truths*, but they never brought *the truth*, to their fellow-men ; for the truth is one, whole and complete, and to bring it was reserved for him, who *has* the truth, because he *is* the Truth. And then, the truths which they brought, those fragments broken from the great body of the truth, how far mingled with falsehoods they were, how much weakened by contradictions, by contradictions in the teaching, by contradictions in the lives, of those that brought them. Extensively, over what narrow regions the spiritual dominion which they wielded, reached; intensively, how few the hearts which owned homage to them, and oftentimes how slight the homage which they owned. But he is the light of the whole world. It is of him as of the natural sun in the heavens, whereof the Psalmist has said, "His going forth is from the end of the heaven, and his circuit unto the ends of the earth, and there is nothing hid from the heat thereof."

Nay, some would make these words to reach further still. A great teacher of the Greek Church is very earnest that we should not limit "the world" here to that world which we inhabit, but should give the word a wider, and, as he believes, its proper extension. Christ is the light, he urges, not of this world, but of all worlds; the unity of that creation of God, whereof this world is only a province, demanding that not man only, but all the hierarchy of heaven, angels, principalities, and powers, should behold the glory of the Father in the Son, that in his light they should see light; so that to refuse or reject him is to put ourselves out of harmony with all creation, with the moral law not of this world only, but of all worlds. I will not at the present pause to inquire whether this extended meaning may be justly given to Christ's language here;— whether he is claiming here to be the light-bringer and light-giver to all creation, as indeed he is; and not to our world alone. The words have a meaning sufficiently august, when we limit them to our own world, which he, the Sun of righteousness, illumines; and this meaning will abundantly occupy us to-day.

But in what senses, it may be asked, is Christ the light of the world? In many. He is the light, inasmuch as the Spirit which proceeds from him, which never would have reached men except *through* him, that Spirit, being a holy Spirit, preserves them in whom he dwells from those sins which cloud the intellect and darken the understanding, quite as surely and effectually as they defile the heart and lay waste the affections. It is the mists of earth, the steam and vapors rising up from beneath, which blot out the heavenly constellations above. Now he prevents these mists from gathering, or scatters them when they are gathered; and thus the entrance of his word giveth light—or, as the Psalmist boldly declared, he had more understanding than the ancients;—and why? because he kept the commandments. Christ is thus the true educator of the intellect of man, inasmuch as he is the only purifier of the heart of man. O brethren, of how many men it is true that they must be better men, holier men, before ever they can be wiser men; that they have been bribed to perverse conclusions of their intellects by the corrupt affections of their hearts, that only through these they have arrived at those;

for God, by an unchanging law of his moral universe, scatters his penal blindnesses as the punishment of our unlawful desires; and that promise of Christ, "If any man will do his will, he shall know of the doctrine whether it be of God"—that promise has its darker side also, upon which it is not a promise, but a threat: If any man will *not* do his will, he shall *not* know of the doctrine whether it be of God.

I do not, of course, pretend to say that there are not kinds of knowledge as much within the reach of the impure as the pure, of the proud as the humble—in which men may make progress, yea, and win the garland, such as it will be, quite irrespective of their moral condition. But so soon as ever a moral element mingles with any study—and how soon it does so, how wellnigh impossible it is, except in the domain of pure science, to keep it aloof—then at once they are at a disadvantage; and the larger this moral element, the nearer the relation which any study bears to God and the knowledge of him, by so much the greater the hinderance they will find.

"Blessed are the pure of heart, for they shall see God;" and each approach to this purity, each advance in it, is a cleansing and brightening of that mirror in which alone the truth, which is God's daughter upon earth, can be discerned; each allowed impurity, be it of the flesh or of the spirit, a tarnishing and darkening of the same, so that it shall give no clear and undistorted image back.

But Christ is "the light of the world" in a yet higher sense, for it is possible to conceive one higher; not merely as preserving clear and pure and undistorted, the medium through which knowledge can be attained; not merely as keeping healthy and single the eye by which it is discerned;—he not merely enables men thus to acquire truth, but he is "the fountain light of all our seeing" by a yet higher title, as he *is* the truth; for he that hath seen him hath seen the Father; and the Father we know is light, and in him is no darkness at all. Such then as the Father is, such is the Son, "light of light;" the light of the world, as bringing into it the true knowledge of God, the light of the knowledge of the glory of God shining in the face of Christ Jesus, and from him reflected upon us. When he came, the people that sat in darkness (and all people sat in darkness, though some in thicker than others), saw a great light; and wherever men loved that light, and came to it, and did not hide themselves from it, there all the foul and hideous forms of superstition and error, which the slime of the earth had gendered, perished at his presence, as in heathen legend the brood of the Python died beneath the glittering shafts of the god of day.

Let me add, too, that Christ being the central person of all time, in whom the history of the old world ended, from whom the history of the new world began, he has, or rather himself is, "the key of knowledge," the key to the right understanding of all mythology, all history, all philosophy, all art, with each other more serious and earnest activity of the mind of man. And they who, casting him aside, or leaving him out, who saying of him, "What is this man more than an other?" seek to enter into the understanding of any of these, are as men that having some hard problem to solve, first deliberately exclude the only right solution, and, this done, perplex themselves endlessly with seeking an explanation which they have themselves rendered it impossible that they can ever find.

In these ways then, brethren, is Christ "the light of the world;" and the promise which he, as such, makes is this, that he who followeth him "shall not walk in darkness, but have the light of life." This walking in darkness, which is the result of *not* following him, what is it? We must not suppose, for the most part, that it is anything which overtakes a man all of a sudden. Little by little, by unmarked insidious approaches, the darkness which is in him (and there is darkness in every man) encroaches on the light, advances its own frontiers, narrows the domain of the light; and then if, as is too often the case, what is once lost is never won back, no gains compensating continual losses, the darkness in the end covers all. To walk in darkness, it is to see the lode-stars of our spiritual heaven, the truths by which we live, going out one by one — to watch them each day waxing fainter and dimmer and remote, with less of comfort, with less of guidance in them, till at length they disappear, and our eyes see them no more; these disappearing lights being not merely the special truths of revelation and of the life in Christ, but all whereby any moral being is sustained in the soul — belief in God, in goodness, in the freedom of the will, in duty, in responsibility, in immortality, in an answer beyond the grave for the things done in the body. To relax our hold on all these, to suffer them one by one to be taken from us, and to feel, it may be, content, well pleased to let them go, this is to walk in darkness.

This surely is the saddest of all, when men thus accept their darkness, acquiesce in it, are better pleased with the darkness in which all may be huddled up, than with the light which shows and searches out all. It is sad enough to have the world, and our own place and meaning in it, as an unsolved riddle to us, the burden of the mystery weighing on us with a weight which sometimes threatens to crush out the life of our spirits. But it is a far sadder thing yet, when all this ceases to be a riddle or mystery to us at all, not because we have read it in the light of faith, not because that has made all things plain, but because we have renounced all hope, all care, all desire to have it solved at all, because we have learned to smile as with superior scorn on the past perplexities of our spirits, on the obstinate questionings, the "What am I?" and "Where am I?" and "Whither am I tending?" which visited us once; and, dismissing all these as the hypochondria of the spirit, have come to regard the world as a convenient feeding-trough, being resolved to make it yield what it can yield after its kind in the shape of pleasures or honors or riches or enjoyments, to shut in our spirits within the limits of these earthly things, to mind them, to acknowledge and trouble ourselves with nothing beyond. This is a cure indeed of the sickness of the spirit; but it is the cure of death: there may be calm now, if it deserve this name, where there were restless agitations before; but it is the hopeless calm of the grave.

Nor may we suppose, my brethren, that darkness, spiritual darkness at least, is a mere absence of light. It is itself an evil power and presence in the soul. There is, and there can be, no vacuum in the heart of man. What the truth does not fill, lies will fill. Who does not obey the one, must obey the other. They are Satan's slaves who will not be Christ's freemen, and in one shape or another they must do his work, and receive his wages. It was boldly said by one of old, "All the way to heaven is heaven"—perhaps over-boldly said, by one who forgot for a moment what life has of burden and of toil even for the faithful man. And yet these words *have* their truth; and being true, they are true also in their converse; and if all the way to heaven *is* heaven, God blessing even now with infinite blessings his servants that walk in that way, so too, which is the same truth on its sadder and its sterner side, all the way to hell *is* hell:

Vestibulum ante ipsum, primisque in faucibus Orci
Luctus et ultrices posuere cubilia Curæ,
Pallentesque habitant Morbi, tristisque Senectus.

In that "*forlorn* old age" how awfully does the great religious poet of Rome put the last terrible touch to his picture; in that single epithet summing up all—the life which is life no longer, the *vita non vitalis*, in which all springs of joys are dried up, in which the man has overlived himself, his joys, and, which perhaps is sadder still, even his sorrows—the life, it may be, which in its outward desolation and abandonment, without honor, without love, is only too faithful an index of that which is within—the life from which all the grace and ornament of life have departed; till he that bears is now weary of it, and desires only to creep by obscure and narrow passages to his grave.

Which of us, my brethren, would have this the end? And yet our lives may only too easily have such an issue as this. Such an issue lies in wait for every one of us. Look around you, and see, of how many who began well, with far other auspices, is there presently occasion to mourn for the defeated promise of their youth, for the spring which no summer followed, for the buds which never unfolded into flowers. You have known some such, who for a time walked, if not with a personal Saviour, yet with high purposes, and no ignoble scheme for their life; but who now have quite gone back from these, and are well-nigh ashamed that they ever entertained them. Surely it is a matter of deepest interest, one which concerns each of us most nearly, to discover where the flaw was, what hindered the orderly development of a spiritual life in them; how it befell that having come out, at least in part, into the light, the darkness overtook them again. The fault and the flaw was here, in the leaving out of that all-important condition which the Saviour puts—"He that followeth *me*, shall not walk in darkness." Communion with a personal God and Saviour, a patient following of him, this is the one condition of indeed coming out of the darkness of nature into the light of grace; and, having come out, the one condition of abiding in that light and not being again swallowed up by that darkness from which we seemed to have escaped

They whom we deplore, forgot this; they set before them, it may be, some lofty ideal for their lives to which they were determined to conform; but it was one of their own fashioning; and they relied for its carrying out on innate forces of their own; and thus the world was too strong for *them*, and not *they* for the world. They had not calculated on the strength, the subtlety, the pertinacity of the opposing forces which it would bring to bear against them. The impulses which first bore them forward to do battle with it, were presently spent and exhausted; they had no power to renew them, and no other to supply their place. Had they leaned upon a higher strength, had their eyes been toward the Lord, had they followed him, then they too, like the warriors of Gideon, might have been often "faint," but, like them, they would still have been "pursuing." The darkness might have gathered round them for a while, but, children of the light and of the day, they would presently have emerged from it again.

"He that followeth *me* shall have the light

of life." Be it ours, brethren, to make this glorious promise our own. For "to have the light of life," what is it? It is to be in fellowship with him who is at once the light and the life of men; and in this fellowship to become more and more a child of light, for whom the darkness is now past, the darkness of a selfish, the darkness of a proud, the darkness of an unholy heart, and for whom the true light now shineth. That light thou mayest make, if thou wilt, more and more thine own, mayest clothe thyself with it, till it be to thee armor of light, at once a sun and a shield, a glory and a defence. Arrayed in this, thou mayest pass unharmed through all the temptations of this world; till thou, being brought at length into a meetness for the inheritance of the saints in light, shalt stand, all unawares it may be, within the gates of that heavenly City, which needeth neither sun nor moon, "for the glory of the Lord doth lighten it, and the Lamb is the light thereof."

# SERMON IV.

## CHRIST THE TRUE VINE.

# SERMON IV.

## CHRIST THE TRUE VINE.

**JOHN xv. 1, 2.**

*I am the true Vine, and my Father is the husbandman. Every branch in me that beareth not fruit he taketh away; and every branch that beareth fruit, he purgeth it, that it may bring forth more fruit.*

IN this image of the vine and the vine branches, the mystical union which is between Christ and his people, the closeness and the reciprocity of it, he in them, and they in him, is set out more distinctly than perhaps in any other figurative language which holy Scripture employs. This union does not lie at all in some of the leading images which are there employed to set forth this relation; as, for instance, in Christ as the good Shepherd, the faithful as his sheep. It is only brought in, as it were by a certain force, into others; as in Christ the living corner-stone, his people the lively stones built upon him: although it is a singular evidence of the manner in which the sacred writers were full of this blessed truth of Christ's innermost union with his people, that in an image so little seeming to favor, or even to tolerate, it as that of the dead stones of the building, it does force its way, and Christ becomes a *living* corner-stone, " in whom all the building *groweth* unto a holy temple in the Lord." Here, however, there is no need of any such forcing. This union lies naturally in the words. It is indeed the truth, which above all other truths the language that our Lord uses, suggests; and which therefore, having these words for our text, will most fitly occupy us to-day.

It needs not curiously to inquire here what was the immediate motive for the selection of this image; whether, as some suppose, a vine had entwined its tendrils round the guest-chamber, where the Lord and his disciples had partaken of their last and ever-memorable meal; or, as others suggest, that, having left that chamber, they were now passing through some vineyards on their way to the brook Cedron and the garden beyond; or that Christ alludes to that famous vine, all of solid gold, with which, as a symbol of the theocracy, Herod had adorned the temple he rebuilt, and silently contrasts himself with it. No one of these suppositions much commends itself to us; they are all, moreover, unnecessary. The Lord required no such suggestions from without. The entire kingdoms of art and of nature lay ever open before his eyes, with all the most secret essences of things, for him to select from their ample treasure-house what best suited his present need, whatever would best embody that spiritual truth which he now was fain to declare.

So far as Christ did receive a suggestion to these words, it was one derived from those many passages in the Old Testament in which Israel, or the people of God, is spoken of under the type and image of a Vine; and in this fact we have the explanation of that "true" ("I am the *true* Vine") which he claims for himself. For whenever he uses this word "true" about himself, or whenever St. John uses it about him, he claims, or it is claimed for him, not so much that he is the true as contrasted with the false, but rather the perfect as distinguished from the imperfect, as differenced from that which falls short of, and only incompletely realizes, its own ideal, only partially fulfils the promise which, according to its name, it made. Thus when elsewhere Christ announces of himself, "I am the true bread that came down from heaven," he does not deny that Moses gave to the people bread from heaven, for "man did eat angels' food;" he only affirms that it was not such that a man might eat thereof and not die; that it was not, as his flesh was, the food and medicine of immortality. So again, when St. John says of him, "that was the true light," he would by no means imply that every other was a meteor or an ignis-fatuus, misleading and betraying, but only that his relation to "the Father of Lights" transcended that of every other, and was indeed absolute and supreme; so that no higher could be conceived.

Exactly in the same way in this "I am the true Vine," Christ does not deny, but rather allow, to Israel the title of God's vine, which is so often given to it in Scripture, as in that 80th Psalm, "Thou hast brought a vine out of Egypt; thou hast cast out the heathen, and planted it;" and again, in another place, "I planted thee a noble vine, wholly a right seed." What he does affirm is, that Israel was not God's *true* vine; that it did not answer, but disappointed and defeated, the expectations and intentions of him that planted it. Israel was an empty vine, bringing forth fruit to itself, and not to him. Elect though that people had been, the salvation of the nations was not, as it might have been, in it; the nations did not, as fruitful suckers, attach themselves to it. The goodly plant which he had planted on the mountains of Israel was turned into the degenerate plant of a strange vine unto him—" the vine of the earth," whose clusters, after infinite long-suffering, were gathered and cast into the great wine-press of the wrath of Almighty God, and trodden there. Still for all this there had been a time when Israel was most really God's vine, just as it was God's son ("out of Egypt have I called my son"); while yet even then it was not his *true* Son, any more than his *true* Vine, inasmuch as it fell infinitely short of all which one name and the other involved.

Christ, then, in that "true" not contrasting himself with the *natural* vine, but, so to speak, with the *moral*, with that which only in part fulfilled the promise of its name, claims for himself to be the single one to whom this title by highest title competed, in whom alone its promise was completely fulfilled; who, trodden in the winepress should yield, as none other had yielded or could yield, the wine that maketh glad the heart of God and men.

I asked you last Sunday to observe the calm yet deliberate self-assertion of our Lord; and I shall not urge this again. You will not, however, fail to note how it repeats itself here. And in further following up of a not dissimilar meditation you will note as well, how all things fairest and loveliest in the natural world are vindicated for himself by him, who is "fairer than the children of men," and who claims all these as weak types and faint reflections of his perfect beauty." Thus the light is lovely, and the condition of beholding all loveliness, and we have heard him saying, "I am the Light of the world." The starry host of heaven presents a spectacle of unequalled magnificence; of this host he singles out the best and brightest for his own, and proclaims, "I am the bright and the Morning Star." Thus, too, the vine being everywhere in Scripture by just right the type of all things fair and gracious and fruitful, he who is altogether lovely appropriates this name also as his own;—"I am the true Vine"—the kingdom of nature being a prophecy of the kingdom of grace; even as the kingdom of grace is a fulfilment of those prophecies of nature; and he who so spake, herein affirming that he is the kingdom of grace realized to the full whatever was faintly shadowed forth by the vine and the vine branches in that of nature.

But what was it, we may reverently ask, which enabled him to speak this language? How is he this true Vine, the root and stock and stem of a new humanity? Is it in his human nature, as the Man Christ Jesus? or is it as he is the Son of the Father, and himself God from everlasting? Neither answer would be perfectly complete. We should answer rather, as he, being God and Man, was one Christ. There needed indeed his Godhead, underlying his manhood, and penetrating it through and through with its own potency and power; else he could not have been life-giving, having life in himself, a divine energy which he communicated to others. But there needed also in him who should be the true Vine, whereof men should be the branches, a veritable humanity as well. Only by sinking himself in our nature, by himself becoming the very root out of which it grew, could he have spread and diffused himself through a race of regenerate renewed men, only by himself becoming partaker of a human nature, could they have become partakers of a divine. Being God, he has his roots in heaven; for the natural order which places the roots below, and the branches above, is here inverted; and from these roots our life is drawn. Being man, he has also what without this manhood he could never have had, his branches upon earth, or men for his brethren. Neither then as God exclusively, nor as man exclusively, is he the true Vine, but as, being God and man, the divine and human are united and married in one Christ.

He proceeds, "And my Father is the husbandman." Here, as so often, Christ's greatness goes hand in hand with his humility, and he himself brings them into closest contact. He who declares himself to be the true Vine, in the same breath declares his Father to be the husbandman—the husbandman, as the place of the words plainly shows, of the whole Vine; not of the branches only, but of the stock and stem as well

Our Lord will by no means exclude himself from his heavenly Father's husbandry; for he too brought his own will into submission to his Father's, drank of the cup which his Father had mingled, was pruned to the quick by the knife of affliction which his Father bore for him as well as for others; in all points learned obedience by the things which he suffered; and only through this, his own obedience to death, became the author of everlasting salvation to all them that obeyed him.

But while Christ thus does not exclude himself from his heavenly Father's husbandry, it is not of himself that he is chiefly speaking, when he says, "My Father is the husbandman;"—of us rather, of the branches, not of the stem; as they need this husbandry far more; the best needing to be pruned, the worst requiring to be taken away. The best, that is the fruit-bearing, need to be pruned. "Every branch in me that beareth fruit, he purgeth [or pruneth] it, that it may bring forth more fruit." There is something very noticeable here, a certain austerity, which we may sometimes mark even in the very promises of God. The fruit-bearing branches, how shall it fare with them? what reward shall they have? They shall be pruned; their too luxuriant shoots shall be checked, which oftentimes can only be done by a far sharper discipline, a far keener use of the pruning-hook, than they would willingly have chosen for themselves. Christ pledges the faithfulness of his Father, that he, the great Vine-dresser, in that his very faithfulness will not leave his own without that chastening which they shall need for their perfection; this chastening being itself a part of their reward. It is one of those mysterious promises, which sound so strangely except to the ears of faith; greatly resembling that other which the Lord made to the two aspiring disciples—" Ye *shall* drink of my cup;" " Ye shall be baptized with my baptism;" drink of his cup of pain, be baptized with his baptism of suffering; which, threat as it would have sounded in carnal ears, was as a promise in theirs; and did not repel, but rather allured and drew them yet closer to him.

And not less significant the intention of this their pruning—" that they may bring forth more fruit," more fruit of faith, of patience, of love. My brethren, of how many of God's dealings with his elect have we here the explanation. We sometimes wonder with regard to some of these, that he should cast them again and again into the crucible of trial; it seems to us as though they were already refined gold. But he sees that in them which we do not see, a further fineness which is possible; and he will not give over, till that be attained. It is just as in a portrait by some cunning artist, which is now drawing near to its completion. Men look at it, and count it perfect, and are well-nigh impatient that the artist does not now withhold his hand, and declare it finished; while he, knowing better, touches and retouches, returns again and again to his work. And why? Because there floats before him an ideal of possible excellence at which he has not yet arrived; but which he will not rest nor be content till he has embodied in his work. It is thus with God and some of his elect servants. Men, seeing their graces which so far exceed those of common men, wonder sometimes why they should suffer still; why they seem to be ever falling from one sorrow to another. But he sees in them that which no other eye can see — the grace which is capable of becoming more gracious still; and in his very faithfulness he will not deprive them, or suffer them to come short, of this. They are fruit-bearing branches, and because they are so, he purges them, "that they may bring forth more fruit." My brethren, how blessed must God's service be, when he can give nothing better to his servants in reward of their obedience, than the ability to serve him more and better; and, if we may safely judge from the analogy of the passage before us, and other like ones, how different must heaven itself be from the anticipation and imagination of carnal men. They seem to think that a certain amount of disagreeable, unwelcome work for God must be here undergone, that so they may be excused and exempted from all work hereafter; we gathering from these Scriptures rather, that heaven is not a ceasing to work for God, but is work in a wider sphere, and in the spirit of a freer, more joyful obedience; according to those wonderful words of the Apocalypse, "His servants shall serve him;" they shall rule over their ten cities in recognition of their ten talents duly laid out: just as on the other hand the penalty of *not* bearing fruit is the not being able to bear, the very capacity of service being withdrawn and taken away.

For we must not leave out of sight this side of our Lord's words: "Every branch in me that beareth not fruit, he taketh away." First, however, observe that "in me"—"every branch *in me;*" for there is the stress of their guilt whom these barren branches represent; inasmuch as there lay the possibility of their fruitfulness. They are branches *in him*, and yet for all this barren and unfruitful; joined to him, and yet not receiving life from him, the channels by which his grace might have been received into their souls being obstructed by sin and unbelief. In their baptisms they were ingrafted upon him;

they were made branches in him; and yet they would not draw life from him; but refusing him, chose rather to draw death from the stock of that old corrupt nature, which they might have now disowned and utterly renounced. Therefore they are "taken away." But, putting the whole of this passage, and not merely the two verses which constitute my text, together, there is a step *before* this in the progress of their doom, "they are withered;" and a step *after* this, "they are burned;" or putting all in their order, they are first withered, then taken away, and then burned. They are withered—the life of their souls, the joy, the hope, the faith, the love, all these dry up. How should they not, when the fountains which should feed them are stopped, or at least all connection with these fountains broken off? What a mournful thing, this withering of which the Lord speaks, and yet how frequent! Strange as it may sound, how many a man has followed himself to his own grave. He is no mourner (would he were, for then there might still be hope), but he is an assister at the grave of his own better hopes and holier desires, of all in which the true life of his soul consisted, which is all dead and buried, though he, a sad survivor of himself, still cumbers the world for a while.

And then the inward separation becomes an outward as well; the withered branch is taken away. It does not retain even in appearance its connection with the vine. A slightest touch will cause it to fall off, for there is no vital coherence, but only external contact, between it and the living stem. The lightest occasion, the most trivial temptation, will be sufficient to bring out the fact that the man has already inwardly fallen away from his Lord, that all vital union between them has ceased.

And last of all, the withered branches are gathered into bundles and burned. No wood so unfit as the vine for any work but its own; as the prophet Ezekiel significantly taught. If not fit for its own work, it is fit for nothing. And therefore " they are burned." Let us leave this doom in the fearful mystery in which God's word has shrouded it. Sufficient to remember, and there may be a fearful analogy to this in the spiritual world, that we do not make fuel of wood than can be turned to any nobler uses and ends; but that we do so without remorse of that from which all these better uses have for ever passed away.

But, my brethren, how shall we gather up in brief for ourselves the teaching which this Scripture contains. Leaving many secondary lessons, we will endeavor to draw its central lesson from it, to urge this, and to ask you to carry this away with you. Christ is the Vine, ye are the branches. It is not that you *may be* branches; but you *are* branches, in virtue of your Christian profession, and that great sacramental act in which you were sealed to Christ, and engrafted upon him. You *are* branches; but branches dead, or branches alive—branches barren, or branches fruit-bearing—branches which he will prune, or branches which he will take away— that is another question; and it is a question which *you* must decide. There are two roots out of which you may grow, from which you may derive your life, the root of Adam, and the root of Christ. The first, the root of Adam, is a bitter root, a corrupt root, and can only impart to you of its own bitterness and corruption. The other, a new root, though indeed the oldest of all, is a sweet root, and you may draw from it of the sweetness it contains. It has indeed been profoundly said, that the whole spiritual history of the world, and of every man in the world, revolves round two men, Adam and Christ, fitly therefore called the first Adam and the second; these being, so to speak, the two poles of humanity, the one a fountain of death to all, and the other a fountain of life, overcoming that death, to as many as will receive life of him. So indeed is it; and the great question for every one of us is this, To which of these will we belong? with which cast in our lot? from which draw the life which we live in this world, the words we speak, the thoughts we think, the deeds we do? To the first, to the old Adam, we *must* belong by natural birth and generation;

to the second we can only belong by grace, by a free act of God's will, by the divine regeneration, by a birth from above, called in Scripture by many and wonderful names—a new creation, a becoming as little children, a passing from death to life, a being translated out of the kingdom of darkness into the kingdom of God's dear Son—and which, availing ourselves of the imagery supplied by the subject before us, we might fitly call, a being broken off from the root of the old Adam, and a being effectually grafted in upon the new. I say *effectually;* for the first initial act of this engrafting, though all-important, though the germ, if duly unfolded, of everything which follows, may yet come to nothing. There are *regenerate* (I use the word in the sense of the Prayer-Book and of the ancient Church), who yet are never truly *renewed;* who stop short at this first act, an act which might have unfolded itself into the whole Christian life, but which does not so in them. There are branches in Christ which yet may cease to be such; and being dead, must be taken away, and gathered into bundles, and burned. See then, I would say, that this regeneration which is once and for all, unfold and complete itself in a renewal, which must be day by day; see that, being branches in him, ye be also branches which he will own, which draw their life from him, which he may prune (for which is there that needs not this?) which he may prune to the quick, but which he shall not take away; which shall bear fruit, and whose fruit shall remain.

And if it be asked by any, How shall we be such? he himself gives the answer, "Abide in me, and I will abide in you." Union with Christ, this is the secret of all fruitfulness. And if again it is asked, How shall we abide? it may be answered, first, by believing that we have been made partakers of Christ; and then by continual acts of faith on him; falling back evermore upon him; hiding ourselves from the stress of temptation, from the storm of trial in the secret of his pavilion—the life we live in the flesh living it by faith in the Son of God—whatsoever we do, doing it in the name and in the spirit of the Lord Jesus. We abide in him by acts of constant and earnest prayer, by the study and devout meditation of his holy Word, by meeting him often in the communion of his Holy Sacrament; even as, in respect of this last means of abiding, it is very noticeable that these words about the Vine and vine branches, this "Abide in me, and I in you, follows immediately in time on the institution of the Sacrament of union, the festival of Christ's blessed body and blood. And so shall he abide in you; and you, who without him can do nothing, with him shall be enabled to do all things; you shall bear *much* fruit; and that, not such fruit as some bear now, grapes of gall to set their own teeth on edge in the end, apples of Sodom, which however fair to look on at the first, shall one day fill their own mouths with ashes and with dust. Oh, brethren, we have surely something better, something wiser to do with our lives than that which so many do with theirs, who spend the first half of those lives in making the other half miserable, in bringing to a baleful ripeness the bitter fruit, which they must themselves hereafter eat in sorrow and confusion, and perhaps in despair.

And if when we invite you to this, the **past** discourages you, past negligences, past sins, past barrenness, so that you have now well nigh no heart to undertake the work set before you, that past, I would say, may indeed humble, but I do not think it need discourage you. You remember, perhaps, the comfort with which the great Athenian orator and patriot sought to strengthen and encourage the spirits of his countrymen in their final struggle with Philip. "If," he used to say, "we had done all that we might, if we had been watchful as we should have been, if we had put forth our strength wisely and well, and yet were in such evil condition as we are, we might then with good reason despair. But seeing we must own that we have not done so, that all this has come upon us because we have been careless, self-indulgent, wanting providence to foresee a danger, and promptness to meet it, there is **a** good hope that if *we* take another course, **our** affairs will take another course as well." Exactly so is it, brethren, with some of us. If we had prayed earnestly, and yet no more had come of it than has come; if we had striven manfully against sin, and yet sin had obtained so great a dominion over us as it has; if we had faithfully fulfilled the conditions of our baptismal covenant, and yet, notwithstanding, had so often and so grievously fallen; if we had sought to abide in Christ, and yet had remained barren and unfruitful as, alas! we are, we might then indeed justly despair; might let our hands hang down, and the stream of our corruptions bear us whither it would; we might drift to our ruin without one effort or one struggle more.

But it has not been so. Things have gone backward with you, because you have been at no pains that they should do anything else; because, without a miracle, such a miracle as you have no right to expect, they could not have done otherwise; because there have been a thousand wastes to your baptismal grace and no replenishings; much outgoing, and little or nothing incoming; because you have prayed little and coldly and formally, or it may be, have not prayed at all; because you have nourished no secret life with God in the reading and meditation of his Word; have forsaken his holy Table, or, if you have drawn nigh to it, have *so* come that you would far better have stayed away than have thus presented yourselves there; because, it may be, by open acts of sin, of uncleanness or other excess, you have inflicted deep gashes upon your souls, and let out their spiritual life-blood, not now in drops but in streams. I say then that in looking back upon all this, if this *is* the retrospect, there is matter for infinite humiliation, but not for inert and inactive despair. Such a life could have had no other issues than it *has* had. But claim, which is your right, to live in God, to live in Christ, to draw life from him; claim all which he freely gave you when he said, "I am the Vine, ye are the branches;" and, whatever the past has been, for the time to come you may yet have "your fruit unto holiness, and the end everlasting life."

# SERMON V.

## CHRIST THE JUDGE OF ALL MEN.

# SERMON V.

### Advent Sunday.

## CHRIST THE JUDGE OF ALL MEN.

#### John v. 26, 27.

*For as the Father hath life in himself, so hath he given to the Son to have life in himself; and hath given him authority to execute judgment also, because he is the Son of Man.*

It is not surely by accident, it is not without its meaning, that our Christian year begins at a different moment from our natural. There is still a full month to run, before another secular year commences; the new Christian year has commenced already. We are thus impressively taught that there are two orders in this world; an order of nature, and in the midst of this, and owning other laws than this does, an order of grace. With Advent Sunday, as a glance at our Prayer-Book is itself sufficient to indicate, our Church year, as distinguished from our natural, begins. We enter this day upon a period which the Church has specially dedicated to the contemplation of the coming of our Lord and Saviour—in which she would have us devoutly carry back our thoughts to his first coming in great humility, to the cradle of Bethlehem, with a few poor shepherds round it; in which She would have us carry on our thoughts to his coming again in his majesty, to the throne of his glory, with thousands and ten thousands of angels waiting to fulfil his commands.

Following then these plain leadings of our Church, I propose a little to occupy your attention to-day with the second of these stupendous events, with that yet in the womb of time, that day as yet unborn, but ever hastening to its birth, which shall be, as Christ and his Apostles ever taught, the great consummation of all things, the winding up of the present age, the clearing of all the ways of God, the complete redemption of his servants, the final destruction of his foes.

And yet I can not conceal from myself the difficulty, I may say the danger, of my subject. We have so often talked and heard talk about a judgment-day, and this with so little of earnest addressing ourselves to the tasks which such a day, rightly believed, would impose upon us, that in just punishment of these hollow unreal words of ours we have come, I will not say to disbelieve in such a day, but so to believe in it that it exercises the very slightest influence on our lives. The glorious retributions of that day do not rouse us to a more active well-doing. The dreadful terrors of that day do not drive us to that one hope of sinners, the Cross of Christ. And this most tremendous reality, when it moves us at all, it is rather in the region of our imagination than in that of our affections or our conscience. Thus, who will not own that he has admired the mighty creations of the painter's or poet's skill, as they have sought to portray that judgment-scene, Christ upon his throne, the elect and the reprobate gathered before him — that he has too often done this, without one thought passing through his mind, "I shall be there, I shall be one of that multitude whom these by their art have summoned before that throne; I shall be standing, not as a spectator, but myself to receive my doom, to be acknowledged or rejected, to be set on the right hand of that throne, or on the left;" — while the still more direct and authoritative statements of Scripture have hardly a more effectual working on our hearts or our lives. I feel this danger, the danger that I may increase this dullness and deadness of spirit in myself and in you, even in the very act of warning and protesting against it, and attempting to dispel it. Yet still in the earnest trust that of God's grace this may not be so, I will not decline the subject; but as I have in each preceding discourse taken for my argument some office or dignity of our Lord, I shall not now depart from my rule, but, as this day suggests, consider the glorious Advent of our Lord and Saviour, or Christ the Judge of all men — at the same time not leaving out, as the Scripture never leaves out, the Judge who is the Saviour as well, the King who is also the Brother, and indeed because a Brother therefore a King.

For you will not have failed, I think, my Christian brethren, often to note the remarkable language of my text. In it our Lord declares that all judgment has been committed to him, that he has received authority to execute judgment, *because* he is the *Son of Man*. At first one might have expected something quite different; one might have expected him to say, that all judgment was committed to him, because he is the Son *of God*, for power belongeth unto God. But it is not so; judgment is his, because he is the Son of Man. Therefore is it, because he is himself man and the Son of Man that he exercises this supreme authority among the children of men. There is a memorable prevision of this in the law of Moses, where God, anticipating the future historical development of his people, and that a time would arrive when they should ask a king, gives certain rules and conditions under which they shall proceed to his election, and this among others: "One from among thy brethren shalt thou set a king over thee: thou mayest not set a stranger over thee, that is not thy brother." The law which God thus imposed upon his people, he observed himself. He set no stranger over the children of men, that was not their brother; but one chosen from among his brethren was judge and king, and is so for evermore.

Most blessed, most comfortable thought for those that in the midst of many weaknesses, many infirmities, of temptations often but not always resisted, are seeking with sincerity of purpose to do his will, to walk in his truth. He was himself taken from among men; he knoweth whereof they are made; he can have compassion on their infirmities, having been himself in all points tempted like unto them; he will temper judgment with mercy; mercy shall rejoice against judgment. But dreadful thought for the faithless and false-hearted, that God shall thus judge the world by *the Man* whom he has ordained;

infinite aggravation of their guilt, and therefore of their doom. A *divine* love men might profess themselves unable to understand, unable to meet with a corresponding love of their own. They might plead that it was something too remote, something lifted too high above the range of their sympathies and affections. But how plead this against a *human* love—against *his* love who sought to draw men to himself, and so to his Father, with cords *of a man?* Oh, what guilt to have stood out against this! It will be that thorn-wounded brow, of which the frown will be so terrible; those nail-pierced hands that shall fall with such a crushing weight upon the sinner. It will be in looking at him who was pierced *for* them, and whom *they* pierced, that the tribes of the earth shall wail.

This then is a first consideration which may well rouse us from a cold and heartless contemplation of that great day—this, namely, that the Judge will be the Son of Man, who, because he is such, will execute judgment among men. But in respect of that judgment itself, let us seek without losing ourselves in details, to seize two or three of its grander features, and so to present them to our minds that they may serve to quicken and strengthen the spiritual life of our souls.

And, first, let us keep in mind that while there are many judgment-days in the world's story, that day is the complement and consummation of them all. In one sense, there are many judgment-days. Every day is such; for Christ is a king now, a judge among the nations, putting down one nation and setting up another; removing the candlestick of some apostate Church; taking away the kingdom of God from these, and giving it to others that shall bring forth the fruits thereof. In one sense, there are many judgment-days, however one may crown and complete them all. It is not for nothing that in the 24th of St. Matthew the destruction of Jerusalem and the end of the world so run into one another that it is almost or quite impossible to draw the line, and say what belongs to one, and what to the other. In all likelihood it never was intended that any such line should be drawn; for that day, while it was the rehearsal of a day yet more terrible, was itself *a* day of doom, even as there *have* been, and probably *will* be many such, before *the* day of doom shall arrive. We walk indeed in a world of judgments, where in every page of story the footprints of the divine righteousness may be plainly traced.

And as it is with nations and Churches, so also with men in particular. How often the life of a man is the judgment of that man. With his own hands he has stricken the garlands of gladness from his brow, and if he walks now discrowned, it is because he has discrowned himself; if threads of darkness and gloom are woven into the inmost tissue of his life, from which for this life at least they shall never be withdrawn, it is he himself that has woven them there. Oftentimes this is so plain that every eye can read it; and often, when it is not plain to others, it is plain to the man himself. He who knows the secrets.of his own heart and of his own life, knows what the worm is that has gnawed at the root of his earthly felicity, and caused it to wither. Like an eagle pierced with an arrow which its own wing had fledged, he too, brought down from his pride of place, can only too well perceive that the arrow of God's judgments which found him out, was fledged and speeded by his own sin.

Yet while thus there are as many judgment-days in the world's story as there are days, God showing even now that he is a God of judgment, and that by him actions are weighed, still for all this how imperfect, how incomplete are they all. How much is left in the rough; how much needing to be adjusted and set on the square; how much is evidently postponed, waiting the redress of a mightier day. The wicked prosper, the righteous are trodden under foot. Dives feasts to the end, and Lazarus pines to the end. The present is oftentimes what St. Paul so significantly calls it, "man's day"—man's, at least, in part; for God, in the language of the Psalmist, "is strong and patient"—patient because he is strong, because he can afford to wait; because none shall through the delay escape from his hands. A day, however, is coming which shall not be man's any more; a day which shall be God's day, God's altogether, which he shall vindicate as wholly his own; that which shall difference it from every other day consisting in this, that it shall be the final and complete adjusting of God's accounts with the world, and with every man in the world; the day which will not leave, as every other day has left, its long arrears behind it; but that wherein every sin which has not been freely forgiven through Christ the Saviour, must be duly punished by Christ the Judge.

Let us not, my brethren, lose sight of this: as little indeed of one as of the other side of this solemn truth. Do not let us in thought of a future judgment, lose sight of a present; do not let us in view of a present, explain away a greater which is in store. We can not afford to let either, or our faith in either, go. A day of judgment far off, with nothing in hand, no present pledges of God's zeal for righteousness, no first-fruits of judgment, would soon be for men little better than a shadow or a dream; and that, " Tush, doth God see?" "the Lord hath forsaken the earth;" "every one that doeth evil is precious in his sight," would soon be the utterance not merely of a few eminently ungodly, but the shuddering apprehension of all. While on the other hand to suppose that all was being judged now, that there was no huge catastrophe in store, no divine crisis in the world's story, larger, mightier, more searching, more satisfying than any that hitherto has been, redressing all which is now unredressed, rewarding all that is now unrewarded, punishing, where this shall need, all that is unpunished now—this were enough to drive a righteous man, as he looks out on the present face of the earth, and the oppressions done under the sun, to despair. Be it ours to keep, by God's grace, a fast hold on both these truths, and to believe in our God as one who both now *is* judging, and hereafter *will* judge, the world in righteousness by the Man whom he has ordained.

But, secondly, it follows from the *final* character of that day, and constitutes another characteristic feature of it, that it shall be one in which God shall judge the *secrets* of men's hearts by Jesus Christ. "We must all *appear*," or, as now it is generally admitted, the words with a slight variation should be rendered, "we must all *be manifested* before the judgment-seat of Christ"—a far more searching thought. If we were to employ a homely expression and say, "turned inside out," it would, I believe, exactly express the intention of St. Paul; all that is inward now, and thus hidden, becoming outward then; all secret things searched out; every mask stripped off; every disguise torn away; whatever any man's work has been, that day declaring it; and not according to its outward varnish, but its inward substance; for it shall be eminently a day of *revelation*, of unveiling, that is, or drawing back the veil which now covers and conceals so much. It shall be a day of revelation, and this in respect of the hidden things both of glory and of shame.

It shall be a day of revelation for the hidden things of glory. We may bless God that there shall be many such, which shall be first unveiled upon that day, the deeds of light, which yet shunned the light as carefully as ever the deeds of darkness have done; the alms which the right hand did, and the left hand never knew; the acts of self-denial unguessed of by all save the doer; the painful victories over self, won in the unseen battle-field of the heart; the prayer of many a Nathanael under the fig-tree; the wrestling of many a Jacob with God as with an adversary through the long night of some strong temptation; all these shall come forth, that he who saw in secret may reward them openly. Nor will that be only a day when God's hidden ones shall first be revealed to others. Many a faithful man shall then first be revealed to himself, shall wonder to find that of the good whereof he thought so little, God has thought so much; and shall hardly understand that for this very reason, namely, that he esteemed of it so humbly, that he forgot it, therefore God has written it in his book.

But seeing, brethren, that there is *nothing* hidden which shall not be known, nor covered which shall not be revealed, that day shall be the day of a sadder revelation, that namely of the unfruitful works of darkness, of the hidden things of shame; and all which the sinner would hardly have borne should be known to one fellow-man and fellow-sinner, which he would have counted no darkness nor shadow of death thick enough to hide now, he must then avouch in the face of an assembled world, before the holy angels, and God the Judge of all. No wonder that we read of some that on that day shall rise "to shame and everlasting contempt;" that shall cry to the hills to cover them, and the mountains to fall on them: who would welcome even this destruction rather than the scorn and confusion which shall then be their portion. No wonder that the Psalmist, looking onward to such a day, should have exclaimed, "Blessed is the man whose sin is covered, whose unrighteousness is forgiven." What man is there among us, who would not fain make his own the blessedness of the man whose iniquity on that day shall be sought and not be found; for he, the same who makes inquisition for it, shall himself have already borne, and borne it away, and abolished it for ever. And here too it shall not be only what men have hitherto concealed from others which shall then be laid bare. Many a sinner shall then first be revealed to himself. The long self-delusion of a life, the flattering of himself in his own eyes, the counting all his ways pure, all this shall only then have end. Surely if this is possible, that a man may hide himself not merely from others, but from his own self, our prayer to God should be, "Show me myself betimes; let me not first discover my sin, my guilt, my misery, when it is too late to part from them, when there is no more sacrifice for sin, when these must cling and cleave to me, and be a portion of myself, for ever."

But then, when all are thus made manifest to themselves and to others, then shall the King divide between them; and to use his own simplest but sublimest words, "separate them one from another, as a shepherd divideth his sheep from the goats;"—then, and not till then; for every mouth must be stopped, and the righteousness of his judgment must be apparent to all. Consider a little what this separation of the precious from the vile must be. Here in the present time light alternates with darkness, good men are mingled with bad; streaks of light partially illumine even the darkness itself; evil men, even though evil be the predominant law of their lives, are not all evil. But there all good will be gathered by a natural affinity to him from whom its goodness first descended: all evil must own what it is so slow to acknowledge now, an Evil *One* as the father from whom originally it came. There are *many* companies now, grouped according to the transient laws and necessities of this present time; there shall be only *two* companies then. In one shall be all the excellent of the earth, all that have kept the faith, that have overcome the world, that have made their garments white betimes in the blood of the Lamb; saints and martyrs that stand forth to us as the pillar fires of that heavenly City toward which we travel; and with these thousands and ten thousands of whom the world keeps no memory, whose names, not written here, shall yet be found written in heaven in the Lamb's book of life. Nor those only of other times, unknown to us in the flesh, or heard of only by the hearing of the ear; but some also for whom we ourselves have thanked God that such have been, and that our lives were blended with theirs; being, as they are to us, the pledge of an eternal life beyond the grave worth all the arguments of the schools, for we are sure that such love, such goodness, could never have been kindled in human souls, again after a little moment to be extinguished for ever. To these the King shall say, "Come; you loved, weakly and imperfectly, yet still you loved him who had first loved you, and now the kingdom of love opens its arms to receive you."

But that other company, the dregs and dross of the world, the refuse and offscouring, all the darkness, the pride, the falsehood, the selfishness, the lust, the cruelty, the hate, all which, isolated and scattered, shows so hideous now, all this gathered into one, unchecked by the presence of any good, fiercer and stronger because then finding no vent, but all turned in upon itself, who can dare to dwell even in thought upon this? They shall be judged already; the being what they are shall be itself their judgment; which judgment shall yet embody itself outwardly in that "Depart from Me" of the King; "Depart from me; ye have chosen to abide at a distance from me, and now take for ever that which ye have chosen. My love toward you awoke no answering love on your parts toward me, nor toward my brethren and yours; and now the kingdom of love rejects you, as ye have rejected it. Be filled with your own doings; be gathered under your own head; under the banner of him who is the prince of lust and selfishness and pride; as I am the Prince of purity, of humility, and love, and would fain have gathered you under mine."

Yet think not, brethren, when we thus speak,

when, as Scripture has done before us, we divide these solemn and dread utterances of Christ into a "Come" and a "Depart," that these are therefore two different revelations of God. They are at the root one and the same, working differently according to the different quality of that on which they work. When we say, "Our God is Love," and when we say, "Our God is a consuming fire," we do but say the same thing over again, looking at it from opposite sides. For just as the same heat hardens the clay and softens the wax, affects each, that is, according to its own nature; or as the same light gladdens a sound eye, but torments a diseased; as the same pillar of a cloud was a cloud and darkness to the Egyptians, but gave light to the children of Israel, guided these, and troubled those; so the same supreme moral energy of God which is at once intensest love of good, and intensest hatred of evil, drawing to itself whatever is akin, repelling from itself whatever is alien, to it, shall work the joy and blessedness of all that through the regeneration have in the ground of their being become like-minded with him, being lovers of good; the tribulation and anguish of all that are contrary-minded, and whom the dreadful presence of that good, from which they shall now be able to hide themselves no longer, shall at once condemn and torment. The revelation of the righteous God, of the incarnate Son of God, contains in itself all which the ungodly can fear, or the faithful can desire.

Let us, I beseech you, try ourselves each one, and estimate our own standing and condition in that kingdom which he shall set up, in the light of this awful fact. Christ shall set up a kingdom of truth: hast thou loved the truth, or hast thou rather been loving and making a lie? He shall set up a kingdom of purity: hast thou been seeking to cleanse thyself from all filthiness of flesh and spirit? or by sensual thought and sensual act polluting both?—of love; but hast thou been selfish and hard-hearted? of humility; but hast thou been proud and high-minded? There shall no wise enter into it *any* thing that defileth. Is this the sentence of thine exclusion?

What questions, my brethren, concern us at all so nearly as these? to be with God, or to be without him for ever, it is this which that day must determine; or rather it is this which that day must declare; we are ourselves *determining* it *now;* that day will only *declare* it. There are indeed who see a light breaking even for them whom that day shall enfold in its darkness; and far, far off, the faint glimmering of another dawn for them beyond the blackness and darkness which shall encompass them now. I can not see it in God's Word, but, on the contrary, very much which excludes it; which proclaims that for them who reject the Gospel of his grace, there remaineth, when once their day of grace has ended, no other sacrifice for sin than that which they have wilfully despised and rejected; and to my mind our life would lose much of its solemn earnestness, its awful meaning, if I did not believe that within those brief limits which shut it in on either side, the issues of eternity were being decided, and we making our choice, that choice which must be ours for ever; choosing for God, or choosing against him; to be ever with Christ, or to be ever separated from him; if I did not feel, brethren, that within these narrow lists, which yet are not too narrow for this great decision, everything must be gained, or everything be lost.

THE END.

www.ingramcontent.com/pod-product-compliance
Lightning Source LLC
Chambersburg PA
CBHW030900170426
43193CB00009BA/687